# WORD SEARCH PUZZLES

## FOR CLEVER Kids

### MARK DANNA

JUNIOR

**PUZZLE WRIGHT JUNIOR**

JUNIOR   New York

An Imprint of Sterling Publishing Co., Inc.
1166 Avenue of the Americas
New York, NY 10036

This Puzzlewright Junior edition published in 2017.

The puzzles in *Word Search Puzzles for Clever Kids* are taken from:
*Word Search Puzzles for Kids* (1999)
*Great Word Search Puzzles for Kids* (1999)
*Totally Cool Word Search Puzzles* (2002)
*Awesome Word Search Puzzles for Kids* (2003)
*Amazing Word Search Puzzles for Kids* (2008)
*Challenging Word Search Puzzles for Kids* (2008)

ISBN 978-1-4549-2280-3

Distributed in Canada by Sterling Publishing
c/o Canadian Manda Group, 664 Annette Street
Toronto, Ontario, Canada M6S 2C8
Distributed in the United Kingdom by GMC Distribution Services
Castle Place, 166 High Street, Lewes, East Sussex, England BN7 1XU
Distributed in Australia by NewSouth Books, 45 Beach Street, Coogee,
NSW 2034, Australia

For information about custom editions, special sales, and premium and
corporate purchases, please contact Sterling Special Sales at 800-805-5489
or specialsales@sterlingpublishing.com.

Manufactured in Canada
Lot #:
2  4  6  8  10  9  7  5  3  1
05/17

www.sterlingpublishing.com
www.puzzlewright.com

# CONTENTS

# INTRODUCTION

**WELCOME TO THE WONDERFUL WORLD** of word searches. (Say *that* three times fast!) Sure, words are used primarily to communicate, but let's face it—they're a lot of fun to play with, too. And there are lots of ways to play with them.

A word search puzzle is like a game of hide-and-seek. We hide the words ... you go seek them. If you've never solved a word search, no problem. We'll explain all the rules shortly. If you have done word searches, keep reading. You'll learn about the twists we've added for some extra fun.

A word search puzzle is made up of two main parts: a grid and a word list. The usually rectangular-shaped grid is filled with what looks to be a meaningless jumble of letters. Actually, that jumble hides all the words and phrases given in the word list, which appears on the same page.

All the hidden words and phrases in the grid go in a straight line—horizontally, vertically, or diagonally. Horizontal words go left or right. Vertical words go down or up. Diagonal words slant. So, if you think about it, words can run in eight possible directions: along the lines of a + sign (the horizontals and verticals) or along the lines of a × sign (the diagonals).

Also, the same letter may be used more than once when words cross each other or overlap. And one more thing to know: ignore all punctuation and spaces in the word list when searching in the grid. For example, "That's all, folks!" would appear in the grid, in some direction, as THATSALLFOLKS. If all that sounds confusing, don't worry . . . it won't be for long. All it takes is a little practice.

You can tackle a word search in many ways. Some solvers start by searching for the across words. Others look for the long words first or words containing less common letters such as Q, Z, X, or J. Still others begin at the top of the word list and methodically work their way to the bottom. Whatever works for you is fine.

The same holds true for marking the grid. You can loop the hidden words (as most people do), draw a straight line through them, or circle each individual letter. Whatever you choose, we recommend you cross off the words on the word list as you find them in the grid.

Each of the 58 puzzles in this book has a different theme and about the same level of difficulty, so you can skip around and do the puzzles in any order you like. Most of the grids are in the shape of a rectangle with 11 letters across and 15 letters down. (That's useful to know. If a word or phrase is more than 11 letters long, it is too long to fit across or diagonally and so it must run vertically.) I've tried to make sure the puzzles here have a good balance of horizontal, vertical, and diagonal words throughout the grid. And there are no isolated words here—except in one special puzzle that you'll see, each word crosses at least one other word, and all the words are interconnected.

This book is special for many reasons. The biggest reason is that there are puzzles within puzzles. In fact, each puzzle contains a hidden message! After you've found all the words in a grid, read the unused letters left to right, row by row, from top to bottom and you'll discover that they spell out a hidden message relating to the puzzle's theme. (There's no punctuation, so figuring out where the punctuation should be is a little bit of a puzzle in itself.) Hidden messages contain silly sayings, puns, riddles, amazing facts, quotations, definitions, or interesting observations. Hidden messages are a bonus you won't always find in other word search books or magazines.

Another puzzle-within-a-puzzle may be the theme itself. Sometimes the puzzle's title will make the theme obvious. Other times, you'll need to use a little imagination to see what the title means. In the three "Guess the Theme" puzzles, you'll really need to use your noggin because you won't be given the themes *or* the word lists!

There are other added twists. A few grids have shapes related to their themes, one has a word list in which all the entries are the same length, and some puzzles are "rebus" puzzles in which parts of the words in the word list are replaced in the grid by pictures or symbols. For instance, in one puzzle, the letters O-N-E in the word list have been replaced in the grid by the digit 1.

None of this should throw you for a loop. *Word Search Puzzles for Clever Kids* is easy and fun for kids of all ages. (Yes, Mom and Dad, that means you, too.) So mark my words—literally! You'll have a great time "Getting Started" with the first puzzle all the way through to the last puzzle, where you'll say "This Is Z End"!

—*Mark Danna*

# "GUESS THE THEME" INSTRUCTIONS

**TO MAKE THINGS A BIT TRICKIER**, the themes and the word lists of three puzzles are a secret. It's up to you to figure out what the 20 items hidden in the grid are and what they have in common. To get you started, we'll tell you the first letter of each word or phrase and give you the appropriate number of blanks. For example, if the item were APPLE TREE, the hint in the word list would be A _ _ _ _ _ _ _ _ .

After you loop an item in the grid, fill in the appropriate blanks below the grid to help you with the word list. If you find a word that doesn't fit in any of the blanks, ignore it: it's not part of the list. If you're trying to think of things that might be in the word list, you may come up with more than one word that will fit a particular set of blanks. But it's better to do that after you've figured out the theme, because then if something you think of doesn't have something in common with all the other entries, you'll know to ignore it. To help you, the clue list, when completed, will be in alphabetical order. There is just one correct overall puzzle solution.

When you're done looping, read the unused letters from left to right, row by row, from top to bottom. They will spell out a message that reveals the theme.

```
R E T S I G E R D T D
N R T Y O I F V E A R
S O S H D A F D O K V
O I I C E A O R E E W
P D L T N G E A G A E
E M N G I H E R R D I
N N E E T D T M T E S
T D B T E F U O R E E
H P I U U P K A D P G
E H T P T R U I I B N
B D E T A E S E B R G
O M E B H K O U K E P
O T M A C I H P L A N
K E I I L N N G C T W
E A P H C T E K S H R
```

AUDITION
BE SEATED
DEAL
EMBARK
ENLIST
GET READY
GET UP
GO HIDE
HIT THE ROAD
OPEN THE BOOK

PACK
PICK SIDES
PLAN
REGISTER
SKETCH
TAKE A DEEP BREATH
TEE OFF
THINK
WAKE UP
WARM UP

```
C U S S B B A S T H R
O R E Y R D R I A H O
M O E M S E I U N S T
B S P A Z S L I S O R
D H E E M R D R O H M
E O E E M E O T U R T
N W E T H P H A N C N
T E A E M P A O S O A
A R E S A I U R I O R
L P E S H L R T A A O
F N T U C C O R Z A D
L E W O T L L O O T O
O H E M D I R O R R E
S O O P M A H S T A D
S K L E E N E X L H S
```

| | |
|---|---|
| BRUSH | MOUSSE |
| COMB | NAIL CLIPPERS |
| CREAM | RAZOR |
| CURLERS | SHAMPOO |
| DENTAL FLOSS | SHOWER |
| DEODORANT | SOAP |
| HAIR DRYER | TOOTHPASTE |
| KLEENEX | TOWEL |
| LOTION | TWEEZERS |
| MIRROR | WASHCLOTH |

```
        W  O  S  N  O  O  P  Y  S  O  D
        S  E  T  I  L  O  O  C  E  O  J
        O  I  K  K  C  K  R  S  C  T  T
     H  E  C  B  P  S  E  I  S  U  N  I  L
     R  U  R  I  M  R  A  D  S  R  T  S  K
     H  P  A  A  U  G  H  L  E  I  E  C  R
  C  C  N  M  N  P  H  I  S  L  T  M  E  A  A
  W  O  O  D  S  T  O  C  K  D  Y  D  E  M  C
  O  S  T  C  H  A  R  L  I  E  B  R  O  W  N
        L  Y  E  E  O  F  A  L  V
        E  R  R  T  L  R  I  A  C
        A  L  G  Y  O  G  H  N  A
        S  H  M  N  C  A  A  K  R
        D  O  G  H  O  U  S  E  K
        S  V  A  N  P  E  L  T  B
```

| | |
|---|---|
| "AAUGH!" | LUCY |
| BEAGLE | MARCIE |
| CACTUS | PIANO |
| CHARLIE BROWN | RED BARON |
| "CHUCK" | RERUN |
| DOGHOUSE | SALLY |
| GREAT PUMPKIN | SECURITY BLANKET |
| JOE COOL | SNOOPY |
| KITE | VAN PELT |
| LINUS | WOODSTOCK |

# "TAKE A HIKE!"

```
W H E T E N S M Y O S
U W S L A R T N A T U
S E O M E E R O N P N
R O C K S V E E T O S
O L R O H T A P I E C
K A T A M V M T E L R
M C R Y O P A U I A E
L L A O N R A M E O E
I T I P D E B S L L N
Q H L Y K K I M S I O
U R H H E C E D A H S
I E E L B M A R C S R
D T A O T A R B T K E
S A D C L E A R I N G
E U G I T A F H I K E
```

| | |
|---|---|
| BACKPACK | PATH |
| CLEARING | REST |
| CLIMB | ROCKS |
| COMPASS | SCRAMBLE |
| DEHYDRATION | SHADE |
| ELEVATION | STREAM |
| FATIGUE | SUNSCREEN |
| LIQUIDS | TERRAIN |
| MAPS | TRAILHEAD |
| MARKERS | TREK |

# LIFE OF E'S

```
E S R E Z E E W T V D
E T F E L E E D E S E
E E L D P E V S R E B
S P E L L E R N E E D
L E E S T E E P L E E
N E S V V E X K E S E
S S S E L H C E E P S
R W E E E R E E H E T
E R N S E H E E W X B
F L N C E G D D E P E
E N E E T N E V E S P
R T T V W H D E R E E
E N E V E E W R H E M
E S T F R E E E T Z E
S E L F E S T E E M S
```

BEEKEEPER
EXCEEDED
FREE VERSE
GEESE
LEVEE
NEEDLE
PEE WEE
REDEEM
REFEREE
SEEDBED

SELF-ESTEEM
SEVENTEEN
SPEECHLESS
SPELLER
STEEPLE
"TEE-HEE!"
TENNESSEE
TEPEE
THREE-WHEELER
TWEEZERS

# THE ROMAN EMPIRE

```
M O U N G T Y O A I N
N I T A L R M W N M A
T R G E A B R U T U S
R O F S D L A J O E J
T M E W I E D U D S O
Y A W N A I P P A I W
C N N S T H F I I L T
L N L U O O V T I O A
N U I L R E N E I C E
A M S U C A T R A P S
O E M M Q U A A E D U
C R T O S H T O N A S
N A E R C C S U M E R
I L E N N T R O D M S
E S E V E N H I L L S
```

| | |
|---|---|
| APPIAN WAY | JUPITER |
| ARMY | LATIN |
| BRUTUS | NERO |
| CAESAR | REMUS |
| CHARIOT | ROMAN NUMERALS |
| COLISEUM | ROMULUS |
| FORUM | SENATE |
| GLADIATOR | SEVEN HILLS |
| IDES | SPARTACUS |
| JUNO | TOGA |

# AT THE BALLET

```
S R E K C A R C T U N
O M E U S F T O E O X
P T B P Q I A T L L U
L A R P L S T R Y E E
P O R P O E E S H O D
C O S T U M E B P T E
T A I O N T A K A A D
E N R N B E U A R R S
T I G H T S R T G D A
P R O L L E E E O T P
S E O H S D E R E H T
T L O L S H E L R P G
E L E T A L M O O A R
E A E I L P O F H L B
P B E X C I B B C L E
```

ARABESQUE
BALLERINA
BARRE
BOLSHOI
CHOREOGRAPHY
CLASS
CORPS
COSTUME
LEAP
LEOTARD

NUTCRACKER
PARTNER
PAS DE DEUX
PIROUETTE
PLIÉ
POINTE
SPLIT
"THE RED SHOES"
TIGHTS
TUTU

For instructions on how to solve Guess the Theme puzzles, see page 7. The word list is on page 66.

```
A S L L A B T H G I E
N L K L T S A H E H L
U I D U S Y D D E N Z
N I U G N E P B N E Z
S T H I O K N A B A U
H E G R O O S R A R P
A E C K P N A C N O D
B A O E Y A W O L N R
I F M O I I R D B E O
T I I D N P M E X G W
M E B O L O S R A C S
C K C M V A A S O N S
D N G I S Y A W E N O
W H E N D I S T E H R
R E G O R Y L L O J C
```

B__ ____
C____ _____
C___
C_____ _____
D___
D_____
E____ ____
J____ _____
M___
N__'_ _____

O__ _____
O__-___ ____
O___
P____
P_____
P____ ____
S____
S_____
X-___
Z____

```
V O P R T I E E I A R
L C A U C U S Y N A T
N C R N D L O S C F V
E T T F L E R N U W A
A S Y O S O A S M E D
L O P R N G A N B D S
P I C O N C E D E N D
O S D F O O M B N E N
L T V F E T A R T V A
I Y A I C T O O O I H
T R R C E U L H P C E
I T U E T L S E P T K
C A M P A I G N O O A
S L E B C T C V I R H
O N H C E E P S S Y S
```

| | |
|---|---|
| BALLOT | POLITICS |
| CAMPAIGN | POLLS |
| CAUCUS | RACE |
| CONCEDE | RUN FOR OFFICE |
| DEBATE | SHAKE HANDS |
| DONORS | SPEECH |
| INCUMBENT | TACTICS |
| ISSUES | TV ADS |
| PARTY | VICTORY |
| PHOTO OPS | VOTE |

Each entry in the list contains the word POINT, but in the grid, each POINT appears as a • symbol. For example, if the phrase FREEZING POINT were in the list, it would appear in the grid as FREEZING•.

```
I  F  •  A  P  •  M  E  N  T  Y
D  O  O  U  K  R  B  E  •  A  S
M  A  T  C  H  •  M  L  L  T  C
F  H  E  Y  O  S  U  B  A  R  N
O  H  T  H  I  B  A  N  M  N  E
C  O  I  L  Y  L  D  I  I  L  K
A  I  L  N  L  •  G  •  C  A  A
L  I  O  •  R  G  E  Y  E  O  T
•  U  P  T  H  N  E  N  D  U  L
P  E  T  W  E  I  V  F  O  •  L
N  I  O  A  T  T  T  •  H  E  E
•  G  N  I  N  R  U  T  W  •  W
O  F  S  •  N  A  O  R  E  E  •
T  S  T  R  E  T  C  H  A  •  D
U  R  I  •  E  S  H  O  E  S  N
```

| | |
|---|---|
| APPOINTMENT | POINTE SHOES |
| BALLPOINT PEN | POINTILLISM |
| CHECKPOINT | POINT OF VIEW |
| DECIMAL POINT | POINT OUT |
| DEW POINT | POINT WELL-TAKEN |
| FOCAL POINT | POINTY HEAD |
| "IT'S NOT POLITE TO POINT!" | STANDPOINT |
| MATCH POINT | STARTING POINT |
| PINPOINT | STRETCH A POINT |
| POINT BLANK | TURNING POINT |

```
H  T  R  U  S  T  F  U  N  D  T
S  O  E  W  C  A  P  N  M  B  P
U  D  T  O  N  E  Y  E  E  G  I
O  O  R  A  L  L  O  D  N  K  G
R  O  A  A  U  E  T  S  O  N  G
E  L  U  N  C  H  M  O  N  E  Y
P  E  Q  O  G  T  B  I  F  A  B
S  C  S  T  G  T  I  W  D  R  A
O  N  C  H  E  C  K  D  O  H  N
R  A  E  K  T  N  H  K  E  I  K
P  W  C  I  S  E  E  A  C  R  T
L  O  A  N  E  C  L  K  N  O  C
P  L  O  M  N  E  E  L  S  G  I
N  L  S  R  O  L  S  L  A  O  E
S  A  V  I  N  G  S  W  L  W  Y
```

| | | |
|---|---|---|
| ALLOWANCE | DOLLAR | POCKETBOOK |
| BROKE | LOAN | POOR |
| CHANGE | LUNCH MONEY | PROSPEROUS |
| CHECK | NEST EGG | QUARTER |
| CREDIT CARD | NICKEL | SAVINGS |
| DEBT | PENNY | TRUST FUND |
| DIME | PIGGY BANK | WALLET |

# FAST JUNK

```
C H I C K E N W I N G
J O K A S E R E S S S
A C Y M T E K H O T E
B H M G P A I H A R S
I E C I C E C R E A M
F E Z B L A O P F T O
D Z G R N K R O U P P
A D S A R E S E C O H
P O T A T O C H I P S
O O C Z U O L H A A O
T D E C N E O F A K T
H L T S O T I R O D E
S E S U D K G A E R E
A S R O N D E S A O H
L T G O L D F I S H C
```

BIG MAC
CAKE
CHEETOS
CHEEZ DOODLES
CHICKEN WING
COKE
DONUT
DORITOS
FRIES
GOLDFISH

HERO
HOT DOG
ICE CREAM
MILK SHAKE
NACHOS
OREO
PIZZA
POP-TART
POTATO CHIPS
PRETZELS

# ART CLASS

```
O M O D E L D A B L D
S S C A L L I R C H D
C K S E E I U T A R D
U E O N E S T H Y W C
L T K N H P A I N T R
P C O W W A N S N E A
T H Y T Y G H T I F Y
U B P O R T F O L I O
R O N A E G E R A L N
E O C B T T O Y A L C
E K U C T T A R T L O
B U U E O P E N C I L
T I L K P L N O L T W
W A H G A T O S I S L
P A S T E L S R I K E
```

ART HISTORY
BRUSH
CLAY
COLOR
CRAYON
DRAW
DRYING RACK
EASEL
GLUE
MODEL

OILS
PAINT
PALETTE
PASTELS
PENCIL
PORTFOLIO
POTTERY WHEEL
SCULPTURE
SKETCHBOOK
STILL LIFE

```
T K H G N I L I A R T
E D C N B U T A A S T
A N R O O S E H Y A J
R U O F L A N I F U Q
H O O P S B T U M I P
L B L E O N U P H E A
L E D R A O B K C A B
E R H A D A G S A A R
S N S U L R N P O E E
N R O L W M I A C C Z
E N K N U D H B N T Z
F A B T O T T U B O U
E A T I M E O U T L B
D O O N O B N N E A E
F R E E T H R O W R M
```

| | |
|---|---|
| BACKBOARD | FREE THROW |
| BLOCK | HOOPS |
| BOUNCE | JUMP BALL |
| BUZZER | LAY-UP |
| COACH | "NOTHING BUT NET" |
| DEFENSE | ONE-ON-ONE |
| DRIBBLE | REBOUND |
| DUNK | TIME-OUT |
| FINAL FOUR | TRAILING |
| FOUL | WNBA |

```
H D E H C N E R F A H
N S F P E H O P L S E
A U I S E S I I R G
I T A L I A N N N U L
N A C N O G A U E S A
I G I J A P A N E S E
A E B W S O H I C I E
R E A N I R A D N A M
K N R H T T I S M N A
U G A A D U E U K P O
H L M M F G R O G E S
T I U R R U R K E S N
L S N E P E R S I A N
O H E D A S G D T S S
P K E N I E E C U H H
```

| | |
|---|---|
| ARABIC | MANDARIN |
| CHINESE | PERSIAN |
| ENGLISH | POLISH |
| FRENCH | PORTUGUESE |
| GERMAN | RUSSIAN |
| GREEK | SPANISH |
| HINDI | TAMIL |
| ITALIAN | TURKISH |
| JAPANESE | UKRAINIAN |
| KOREAN | URDU |

Each word in the list is paired with its opposite. For example, BOYS in the left column is opposite GIRLS in the right column. Opposites appear in opposite halves of the grid, so if BOYS is in the top, GIRLS is in the bottom. You must figure out which half each appears in. For good measure, the word OPPOSITES appears equally in both halves.

```
                W
              D O O
            B N T L L
          N M R O M A L
        T T U U P R S R O
      H I E D N P A T K G H
    D B O Y S L O W I H F E F
                S
    T S A F Q U I E T F S E R
      E S M A R T D I L O S
        C O O L E R R N M
          T U I S I S A
            B T G E L
              A H L
                D
```

## OPPOSITES

| | |
|---|---|
| BOYS | GIRLS |
| FAST | SLOW |
| FIRST | LAST |
| LARGE | SMALL |
| LOUD | QUIET |
| NORTH | SOUTH |
| SMART | DUMB |
| SOLID | HOLLOW |
| TRUE | FALSE |
| WARM | COOL |

```
G M Y S T E R Y N A S
N N C A Y D C R E S C
W L I A R T D L O C E
H L I R S S T R U I N
L T L Y R L C A S E E
N S U S P E C T O O O
A U N E L A H G L A F
N F T B L D E D V R T
C S U E V S E I E N H
Y O T Y Y E C E A R E
D E T E C T I V E R C
R S S M I S S I N G R
E U O M L V I T N G I
W C S H E R L O C K M
A S R E D R U M E S E
```

| | |
|---|---|
| CASE | NANCY DREW |
| CLUE | RED HERRING |
| COLD TRAIL | RUSE |
| DETECTIVE | SCENE OF THE CRIME |
| DOUBLE CROSS | SHERLOCK |
| LEADS | SLEUTH |
| MISSING | SOLVE |
| MOTIVE | SUSPECT |
| MURDER | TAIL |
| MYSTERY | VICTIM |

```
Y O C S E L D N A C D
P U L H F A V O R H E
O A O V I E A I A S C
N O W O R G O T E N O
Y T N B S I S A R O R
R T A H T D A T Y O A
I I A B S T F I G L T
D P C E L N D V E L I
E L K E I E A N N A O
S A C H C A C I P B N
C T R U E R K L I L S
T E P H E P E R O E E
H S I W A E K A M T S
A N E N A R T A M H H
T I M E T O G O D A Y
```

BALLOONS
CAKE
CANDLES
CLOWN
CUPS
DECORATIONS
FAVOR
FIRST SLICE
GAMES
GIFTS

HATS
ICE CREAM
INVITATION
"MAKE A WISH"
NAPKIN
"... ONE TO GROW ON"
PLATES
PONY RIDES
TABLECLOTH
"TIME TO GO ..."

# ONE OF A KIND

Each entry in the list contains the word ONE, but in the grid, every ONE becomes a 1. For example, if the phrase ONE AT A TIME were in the list, it would appear in the grid as 1ATATIME.

```
            T  1  Y  A  B
         1  A  S  E  1  A
      D  T  I  A  1  R  W
   E  T  E  L  E  P  H  1
   A  E  Y  L  B  L  A  T  D
F  1  N  O  1  1  1  C  T  I
            L  1  L  O  C
            O  A  A  B  E
            V  Z  B  1  C
            O  L  1  T  R
            R  I  N  L  E
            P  1  S  T  A
D  1  S  I  O  P  S  Y  E  M  Y  A  K  I  N
R  E  1  I  P  I  S  N  B  C  B  E  G  1  D
1  1  F  O  R  T  H  E  M  1  Y  S  R  I  A
```

| | |
|---|---|
| AL CAPONE | ONE-ON-ONE |
| BALONEY | OPPONENT |
| BAYONET | OZONE LAYER |
| BEGONE | PIONEER |
| COLONEL | POISONED |
| HONEST | PROVOLONE |
| ICE CREAM CONE | TAILBONE |
| LIONESS | TELEPHONE |
| ONE BY ONE | THRONE |
| ONE FOR THE MONEY | TONE-DEAF |

```
S  P  N  O  M  F  S  R  E  B  O
Y  I  A  O  T  T  F  E  R  R  Y
N  H  A  M  E  E  S  I  A  R  R
E  S  G  A  N  L  O  R  K  E  E
A  R  M  N  H  S  L  R  L  S  M
A  E  L  R  I  K  Y  A  W  L  M
R  P  T  I  I  D  H  C  G  T  A
S  P  S  C  O  W  A  T  N  I  J
C  I  C  C  P  F  A  F  B  N  D
H  L  T  U  G  B  O  A  T  T  N
O  C  N  T  D  G  R  R  H  I  I
O  T  T  T  L  G  L  C  D  I  W
N  G  A  E  E  N  A  R  S  Y  M
E  I  N  R  K  Y  N  I  O  W  H
R  R  E  N  I  L  N  A  E  C  O
```

| | |
|---|---|
| AIRCRAFT CARRIER | PUNT |
| BARGE | SCHOONER |
| CLIPPER SHIP | SCOW |
| CUTTER | SKIFF |
| DINGHY | STEAMER |
| FERRY | TUGBOAT |
| GALLEON | WHALER |
| HYDROFOIL | WINDJAMMER |
| KETCH | YACHT |
| OCEAN LINER | YAWL |

# HINKY PINKIES

Hinky Pinkies are two-word rhyming phrases in which each word has the same number of syllables. A simple example is DAN RAN. But we think more variety adds more fun, so in the list below, each word in the pair is spelled significantly differently from the other.

```
B  I  T  E  K  N  I  G  H  T  M
K  L  O  Y  E  K  O  P  O  Y  G
T  O  C  T  A  W  S  W  U  Y  S
G  A  V  S  E  E  D  T  N  E  P
H  A  E  E  O  O  E  M  I  U  O
O  T  K  U  U  W  Z  T  O  S  N
D  E  H  G  I  S  E  D  I  U  G
Y  B  H  D  S  Z  E  M  E  E  Y
A  A  J  E  I  U  R  I  O  S  B
K  I  C  S  E  A  F  A  N  E  U
S  T  D  S  T  H  S  E  T  W  N
T  B  E  E  I  A  A  D  R  E  G
A  E  U  L  C  W  E  N  E  S  E
X  C  I  B  A  B  S  R  E  R  E
B  E  R  E  T  A  R  R  A  Y  F
```

| | |
|---|---|
| ATE BAIT | OWE MOE |
| BERET ARRAY | POKE YOLK |
| BET DEBT | SEAS FREEZE |
| BITE KNIGHT | SIZE TIES |
| BLESSED GUEST | SPONGY BUNGEE |
| FRED SAID | SUE'S EWES |
| GUIDE SIGHED | SWAT COT |
| I LIE | TOW DOUGH |
| NEW CLUE | WEE KEY |
| NUN WON | YAKS' TAX |

# IN WONDERLAND

```
T  E  L  T  R  U  T  K  C  O  M
D  W  T  D  I  N  N  K  L  E  A
T  U  W  A  E  I  N  K  L  E  R
T  A  C  E  R  I  H  S  E  H  C
E  L  U  H  N  T  I  W  T  Y  H
S  Q  T  R  E  L  S  H  E  T  H
U  B  A  E  D  S  T  I  H  R  A
O  O  W  H  R  E  S  T  I  A  R
M  A  D  H  A  T  T  E  R  P  E
R  W  L  T  G  O  N  R  D  A  H
O  E  M  I  H  K  N  A  V  E  A
D  E  R  W  C  A  W  B  H  T  K
A  O  T  F  Y  E  N  B  O  U  O
R  E  D  F  L  A  M  I  N  G  O
A  C  R  O  Q  U  E  T  D  T  H
```

| | |
|---|---|
| ALICE | HOOKAH |
| CHESHIRE CAT | KNAVE |
| CROQUET | MAD HATTER |
| DINAH | MARCH HARE |
| DODO | MOCK TURTLE |
| DORMOUSE | "OFF WITH HER HEAD!" |
| DUCHESS | QUEEN |
| "EAT ME" | TARTS |
| FLAMINGO | TEA PARTY |
| GARDEN | WHITE RABBIT |

```
A R T H U R E T S E L
C A R L O S U O H E B
B E R N I E O P U Y W
H Y A R R U M M E A T
Y L Y E V R A H A R B
D E N N I S I V A R T
A N N U N A I L U J H
N O A D G V R N C I O
I I S L I S U C R A M
E L I C O S T T H B A
L U T H E R I E R I S
H O R O F M B Y V O E
R Y U E D U A L C E S
N A C M E N A M R O N
S W A L T E R N E S T
```

| | | |
|---|---|---|
| ARCHIE | ERNEST | ROLAND |
| ARTHUR | HARVEY | RONALD |
| BERNIE | IRVING | RUPERT |
| BRYANT | JULIAN | SAMUEL |
| CARLOS | LESTER | SIDNEY |
| CLAUDE | LIONEL | STEVEN |
| CURTIS | LUTHER | THOMAS |
| DANIEL | MARCUS | TRAVIS |
| DENNIS | MURRAY | VICTOR |
| DMITRI | NORMAN | WALTER |

For instructions on how to solve Guess the Theme puzzles, see page 8. The word list is on page 66.

```
T H E R T H I N K E R
P U Z O I Z L E E T E
K A R T I L L E R Y D
C B T A H U E O M E L
U E R R D H T E A R U
R E I E S T R H I D O
T N H G A M A E R C B
G C S I T T E H I F A
S T A R R E H F A R S
E B S F M O F I C E P
X I U E L A H W N I A
A T T R R E D P A G W
T A I T D T H N E H B
L E I N G E O H E T A
L L A F W O N S V Y S
```

A _ _ _ _ _ _ _ _
B _ _ _ _ _ _
B _ _ _ _ _ _ _ _
B _ _ _ _ _
C _ _ _ _
F _ _ _ _ _ _
H _ _ _ _
H _ _ _ _ _
L _ _ _
M _ _ _ _

P _ _ _ _
R _ _ _ _ _ _ _ _ _ _ _
S _ _ _ _ _ _ _
S _ _ _ _ _ _ _
S _ _ _
T _ _ _ _
T _ _ _ _ _ _
T _ _ _ _ _ _
T _ _ _ _
W _ _ _ _

# "HAIR WE GO!"

```
Y A D R I A H D A B H
U A M M A M S N H A S
I R R G T H O R O T L
W E S P A U T U I W I
P E N M S T C A S Y C
P E P R C R L Z E S K
B O B B Y P I N Z N E
O T E F S A A A S U D
T K A E A R T I H N B
T A D H L E Y S U M A
B E S W O R N R O C C
M R E W N R O T T U K
H T A E K I P S R A N
I S N I W I N L T A E
H A I R D R Y E R R P
```

BAD HAIR DAY
BEADS
BOBBY PIN
BRAID
BUZZ CUT
CORNROWS
CURLY
HAIR DRYER
HAIR SPRAY
MOUSSE

PART
PERM
PLAITS
PONYTAIL
SALON
SHAMPOO
SLICKED BACK
SPIKE
STREAK
WASH

# SNOWBOARDING

```
T  H  E  B  T  F  E  E  R  M  S
F  H  A  N  D  P  L  A  N  T  K
O  R  S  P  R  A  Y  I  S  M  C
G  A  M  L  I  L  T  L  P  Y  I
O  U  U  R  O  H  S  N  G  N  R
J  S  E  N  E  P  E  O  V  W  T
T  A  I  L  W  H  E  E  L  I  E
B  O  M  A  R  D  R  S  A  E  L
R  E  T  S  S  T  F  I  S  S  G
T  S  U  P  E  R  P  I  P  E  G
G  G  R  R  V  S  O  M  E  M  O
E  L  N  A  T  S  S  O  N  R  G
G  R  I  B  I  N  D  I  N  G  S
O  L  N  D  M  S  F  O  O  R  S
H  O  G  R  E  I  K  A  F  N  T
```

| | |
|---|---|
| AERIAL | HELMET |
| ASPEN | INVERT |
| BINDINGS | JAM SESSION |
| FAKIE | JUMP |
| FLIP | SLOPES |
| FREESTYLE | SUPERPIPE |
| GLIDE | TAIL WHEELIE |
| GOGGLE | TRICKS |
| GRAB | TURNING |
| HANDPLANT | VAIL |

```
C O R D U R O Y S W E
A A S R S I S N G E S
X P R S B L O U S E W
S R E G G U H P I H E
E R X N O S I T V T A
D E O C A P R I S M T
C L B O O T A H I E S
S P D O V E S N N T H
M O O E A E I J T N I
J T H T S S R A A S R
B E L T K V I C I N T
G B A I C N G K O O O
D U R N O T A E A A S
T T E I S H N T T H T
S G N I K C O T S E M
```

| | |
|---|---|
| BELT | KHAKIS |
| BLOUSE | MINISKIRT |
| BOXERS | OVERCOAT |
| CAPRIS | SOCKS |
| CARGO PANTS | STOCKINGS |
| CORDUROYS | SUIT |
| DRESS | SWEATSHIRT |
| HIPHUGGERS | TANK TOP |
| JACKET | TIES |
| JEANS | TUBE TOP |

# MARCHING BAND

```
T  I  N  T  U  N  E  E  H  N  O
S  T  R  U  M  P  E  T  O  H  E
G  W  H  U  N  O  D  T  U  A  O
L  N  L  T  O  I  A  E  T  L  K
O  O  E  E  B  F  R  P  F  F
C  P  E  N  O  B  M  O  R  T  A
K  C  E  I  M  A  Y  J  R  I  H
E  P  A  R  A  D  E  A  E  M  E
N  A  R  A  A  D  S  M  I  E  C
S  F  S  L  A  B  M  Y  C  S  I
P  N  F  C  S  E  U  R  R  H  T
I  D  R  A  U  G  R  O  L  O  C
E  E  X  O  N  T  D  W  D  W  A
L  E  R  U  H  M  M  S  E  R  R
S  O  U  S  A  P  H  O  N  E  P
```

| | |
|---|---|
| BATON | IN TUNE |
| CLARINET | MAJORETTE |
| COLOR GUARD | PARADE |
| COLUMN | PRACTICE |
| CYMBALS | ROWS |
| DRUMS | SAXES |
| FLUTE | SOUSAPHONE |
| GLOCKENSPIEL | TROMBONE |
| HALFTIME SHOW | TRUMPET |
| HORNS | UNIFORM |

# SEEING STARS

```
D  S  U  I  R  A  U  Q  A  I  B
F  U  T  U  R  E  D  Y  O  U  U
R  B  C  B  E  A  O  C  L  W  D
Y  O  I  U  N  O  I  L  R  H  R
R  L  D  R  H  O  P  R  O  A  O
A  S  E  C  T  O  R  R  P  T  B
D  E  R  I  T  H  O  S  A  S  Y
N  S  P  P  I  S  C  E  S  Y  D
E  O  N  Z  C  T  S  H  B  O  E
L  L  I  O  E  I  V  E  A  U  A
A  E  P  D  N  V  V  E  R  R  Y
C  E  T  I  H  N  I  I  S  T
G  U  M  A  R  C  H  E  R  I  Y
O  E  S  C  U  R  S  E  A  G  D
G  C  A  P  R  I  C  O  R  N  O
```

| | |
|---|---|
| AQUARIUS | GEMINI |
| ARCHER | HOROSCOPE |
| ARIES | LIBRA |
| BIRTH CHART | LION |
| BULL | PISCES |
| CALENDAR | PREDICT |
| CAPRICORN | SCORPIO |
| CRAB | VIRGO |
| CUSP | "WHAT'S YOUR SIGN?" |
| FUTURE | ZODIAC |

```
M O S K V R O O M T T
T S E T G N I V I R D
R Y R I I D O C A D E
S I R M A R K A C G R
T G D R E E E S O I E
R A I E T N T C N I V
A S E P H E D S V C I
F M E S E O U N E E R
F O N R K R M Y R L D
I N S E A C E E T L T
C E S N E E A W I P O
J Y C R X T H B B H C
A E C A U E X R L O O
M N M E E H O I E N T
D A Y L I C E N S E S
```

BACK SEAT
CELL PHONE
CONVERTIBLE
DRIVER ED
DRIVING TEST
EYE EXAM
GAS MONEY
INSURANCE
KEYS
LEARNER'S PERMIT

LICENSE
RADIO
RIDE HOME
SIXTEEN
STEERS
TICKET
TIRE
TRAFFIC JAM
"VROOM!"
WHEE

```
S R E W O L F P A F S
M P A R N P B O O E F
W O A R D L S A L R N
D I N D O A F B O T C
N T O S E N A R F I D
E A S E D T S I U L L
S O C L E I I K E I A
M G A G R N D E O Z T
W N E F N G D S E E D
E V S O W I N G U R L
E W L O G F R W S E P
D E O G D S B E K A R
I Y I R M O O T T H E
N N R G M H O C O A S
G E S U N S H I N E W
```

| | |
|---|---|
| BLOSSOM | RAKE |
| CROP | SEED |
| DIGGING | SOIL |
| FERTILIZER | SOWING |
| FLOWERS | SPADE |
| FRUIT | SUNSHINE |
| HOES | VEGETABLES |
| PATCH | WATERING CAN |
| PLANTING | WEEDING |
| RAIN | WORMS |

```
            T  P  O  R  T  H  O  L  E
         O  I  U  T  H  E  L  T  R  R  T
      O  Z  U  N  N  D  A  T  H  A  I  E  N
   G  Z  H  U  L  A  H  O  O  P  S  E  G  A  L
   A  R  E  W  H  E  E  G  L  S  G  B  R  U  L
   L  E  S  U  O  R  A  C  U  G  B  B  A  W  A
   L  E  C  S  W  P  O  L  Y  O  N  L  T  K  B
   A  D  D  A  R  T  B  O  A  R  D  I  Y  O  T
   T  S  I  P  F  I  L  W  E  S  S  C  R  O  A
   O  S  L  O  P  K  S  N  O  G  F  I  E  C  E
   T  R  R  E  C  R  C  N  L  E  A  M  H  L  M
   S  R  A  E  E  S  U  O  M  Y  E  K  C  I  M
      F  J  N  R  I  B  S  L  S  B  R  R  E
         E  S  G  E  A  E  N  C  I  D  A
         B  U  E  T  T  O  C  N  S
```

| | |
|---|---|
| ARCHERY TARGET | HULA-HOOP |
| CAROUSEL | JAR LID |
| CIRCLE | MEATBALL |
| CLOCK FACE | MICKEY MOUSE EARS |
| CLOWN NOSE | ORANGE |
| DARTBOARD | PIZZA |
| DOUGHNUT | PORTHOLE |
| EGG YOLK | RING |
| GLOBE | WAIST |
| HALO | WREATH |

# "A-MAZE-ING!"

First, loop all the hidden words to form the walls of a maze. Then enter the maze in the upper left corner and draw a path that crosses only through unused letters until you exit at the lower right. Read the letters along the correct path to find the hidden message. Note: All entries run across or down. No words run diagonally or intersect.

```
I F Y O U G O I N H K
E N T E R O T P R E C
T G N O L A U U E L U
H Y K A N S R K Y O T
I X G I G H N C O S S
S D N R B T D A U T E
P E I E L Y I B L L B
A A T H O A R O H N O
T D S T C W E C T I O
H E I N K G T R A P N
Y N W I E N N O D O S
O D T O D O T L L A W
U L L G O R S T O P N
H E L P T W D N I W O
E Z A M H E T I X E W
```

"BACK UP!"
BLOCKED
DEAD END
ENTER
EXIT
"HELP!"
LOST
MAZE
"OH, NO!"

SNAKY
STUCK
TRAP
TURN
TWISTING
WALL
WIND
WRONG WAY

# BEDTIME

```
A  T  R  I  H  S  T  H  G  I  N
T  S  L  U  N  M  E  I  B  E  L
T  R  T  O  S  P  I  A  R  S  I
A  R  O  T  T  I  U  A  E  E  E
K  Z  S  S  E  U  Q  W  I  Y  D
E  T  S  S  E  M  O  A  O  E  O
A  R  A  E  H  F  R  K  U  R  W
N  N  N  T  S  E  O  E  N  U  N
A  S  D  W  B  E  D  R  O  O  M
P  T  T  M  O  A  Y  O  U  Y  C
P  D  U  K  B  L  A  N  K  E  T
L  L  R  A  T  E  L  S  T  S  H
S  A  N  E  A  N  T  I  E  O  O
D  S  L  U  A  M  B  R  P  L  E
R  A  L  A  R  M  C  L  O  C  K
```

| | |
|---|---|
| ALARM CLOCK | PILLOW |
| AWAKE | QUIET |
| BEDROOM | REST |
| BLANKET | SHEETS |
| CLOSE YOUR EYES | SLUMBER |
| CONK OUT | SNOOZE |
| DARK | SNORE |
| DREAM | TAKE A NAP |
| LIE DOWN | TIRED |
| NIGHTSHIRT | TOSS AND TURN |

```
S  T  L  I  C  F  E  L  I  S  B
T  N  H  I  S  F  A  M  I  L  Y
N  O  S  G  K  D  T  A  E  F  F
E  U  E  A  I  I  N  S  R  B  E
M  E  I  T  N  L  S  E  V  O  L
O  H  R  A  D  I  N  C  I  K  F
M  U  O  T  N  H  L  O  F  R  O
D  R  T  G  E  W  H  N  A  T  F
E  P  S  A  S  A  Y  D  O  S  O
R  U  L  H  S  H  C  C  E  A  O
A  T  R  E  T  L  E  H  S  V  D
H  E  A  M  H  N  T  A  E  D  D
S  O  R  T  H  O  E  N  B  R  E
S  A  T  Y  L  O  P  C  U  C  S
W  A  N  C  F  R  E  E  D  O  M
```

| | |
|---|---|
| A SECOND CHANCE | KINDNESS |
| BLESSINGS | LIFE |
| CLOTHES | LIGHT |
| FAMILY | LOVE |
| FOOD | MUSIC |
| FREEDOM | SHARED MOMENTS |
| FRIENDS | SHELTER |
| HEALTH | STORIES |
| HELP | TEACHERS |
| HOPE | WARMTH |

# LOOKIN' GOOD

```
I  F  E  R  Y  B  O  U  M  I  R
M  A  Y  B  E  L  L  I  N  E  S
A  S  E  A  C  D  O  U  F  S  M
E  E  B  T  I  C  W  F  S  S  Q
R  O  R  R  I  M  U  O  U  H  E
C  I  O  Z  M  B  D  O  P  Y  M
R  O  W  O  D  A  H  S  E  Y  E
E  E  P  G  L  O  S  S  U  H  R
N  G  E  U  A  V  E  C  T  O  Y
I  D  N  T  F  R  N  A  A  K  B
L  U  C  O  E  F  O  E  A  R  O
E  M  I  V  P  M  I  Q  A  K  A
Y  S  L  I  P  S  T  I  C  K  R
E  O  E  U  P  I  O  T  E  S  D
N  A  I  L  P  O  L  I  S  H  T
```

| | |
|---|---|
| BLUSH | MASCARA |
| BUFFER | MAYBELLINE |
| CREAM | MIRROR |
| EMERY BOARD | NAIL POLISH |
| EYEBROW PENCIL | POWDER |
| EYELINER | PUFF |
| EYE SHADOW | Q-TIP |
| GLOSS | REVLON |
| LIPSTICK | SMUDGE |
| LOTION | SPONGE |

# FOOTBALL FUN

```
Y M G O A L L I N E O
O M S S F E T Y P E A
B R R N S T L E H O C
R E E O M O P D V S A
E H D T F R V E D Q T
T I A E A I R W E U C
A D E L T T N F L A H
W V L S I H O U W R F
I Y R M N F F T H T A
E E E R E F E R U E C
S S E I O O B S T R E
H K H K E D S L U B M
U P C P U N T S O A A
E I R A B A H O W C S
K L H A S H M A R K K
```

| | |
|---|---|
| BLOCK | OVERTIME |
| CATCH | PEP RALLY |
| CHEERLEADERS | PUNT |
| FACE MASK | QUARTERBACK |
| GOAL LINE | REFEREE |
| HALF | RUSH |
| HAND-OFF | SACKS |
| HASH MARK | THE NFL |
| HUDDLE | UNIFORM |
| KICKOFF | WATERBOY |

```
I  N  B  S  H  S  P  A  K  E  E
S  P  O  C  U  R  T  A  I  N  M
T  E  W  C  O  A  R  A  E  S  O
N  T  S  P  O  T  L  I  G  H  T
E  H  S  E  A  S  G  E  M  E  I
L  E  E  R  N  N  T  P  L  G  O
A  A  A  F  Y  E  E  U  N  D  N
T  T  S  O  A  C  C  I  M  L  M
L  E  T  R  O  H  T  S  E  E  U
D  R  A  M  A  C  L  U  B  P  S
A  R  E  A  A  E  T  S  T  D  I
S  D  H  N  E  M  H  A  A  L  C
Y  T  E  C  U  S  H  E  R  S  A
A  N  E  E  D  F  L  E  R  M  L
A  L  E  S  U  A  L  P  P  A  E
```

| | |
|---|---|
| ACTING | PERFORMANCES |
| APPLAUSE | PROPS |
| BOWS | REHEARSAL |
| COMEDY | SCENE |
| COSTUMES | SETS |
| CURTAIN | SPOTLIGHT |
| DRAMA CLUB | STAGE |
| EMOTION | TALENT |
| LEADS | THEATER |
| MUSICAL | USHERS |

# SHOE THING

```
I  P  L  A  T  F  O  R  M  S  T
M  V  H  D  L  O  A  F  E  R  S
E  A  L  I  S  D  A  M  O  A  E
S  N  R  D  G  C  S  P  O  S  I
R  S  E  A  O  H  K  P  N  C  P
E  K  K  S  D  C  H  E  M  H  P
K  A  D  E  O  M  K  E  O  U  U
A  R  K  R  C  E  O  T  E  H  P
E  I  A  L  M  H  B  N  A  L  H
N  E  D  D  A  M  E  V  E  T  S
S  T  H  A  R  W  E  R  C  O  U
A  U  I  S  T  A  R  L  S  N  H
D  V  P  A  E  I  O  I  R  S  O
A  F  E  S  N  G  H  O  A  E  S
K  C  O  T  S  N  E  K  R  I  B
```

| | |
|---|---|
| ADIDAS | NIKE |
| AIRWALK | PLATFORMS |
| AVIA | PUMPS |
| BIRKENSTOCK | REEBOK |
| CLOGS | ROCKPORT |
| DOC MARTENS | SKECHERS |
| HIGH HEELS | SNEAKERS |
| HUSH PUPPIES | STEVE MADDEN |
| KEDS | TEVA |
| LOAFERS | VANS |

```
L  L  A  B  T  F  O  S  E  G  G
A  L  G  A  O  O  I  T  N  N  M
L  I  D  S  T  N  A  I  I  I  E
L  R  A  K  N  M  L  W  W  D  M
A  D  P  E  I  W  O  S  W  A  U
B  L  T  T  O  R  L  R  S  E  L
T  T  L  B  A  S  E  B  A  L  L
O  U  O  A  G  S  E  S  T  R  A
O  H  E  L  T  R  A  O  B  E  B
F  I  E  L  D  H  O  C  K  E  Y
A  L  I  D  S  O  N  C  E  H  E
P  N  O  A  U  L  A  E  L  C  L
G  S  U  G  A  R  P  R  A  R  L
T  Q  Y  R  T  N  U  O  C  X  O
S  C  I  T  S  A  N  M  Y  G  V
```

| | |
|---|---|
| BASEBALL | SOCCER |
| BASKETBALL | SOFTBALL |
| BOWLING | SQUASH |
| CHEERLEADING | SWIM |
| DRILL | TENNIS |
| FIELD HOCKEY | TRACK |
| FOOTBALL | ULTIMATE |
| GOLF | VOLLEYBALL |
| GYMNASTICS | WRESTLING |
| ROWING | X-COUNTRY |

# HARRY POTTER

```
Q T N W H S E R E A G
U R A S N A P E E O S
I N B E V E N E B H U
D I A G O N A L L E Y
D N K D R E E H D L W
I R Z A Y T M A S T H
T V A O C U O G M C E
C O H O G W A R T S R
H L M G B I T I A O M
F D L O U P W D W L I
S E C R E T U L I I O
S M N A Q U I C Z C N
S O R T I N G H A T E
I R C I G A M R R D D
I T T C H G D A D M E
```

| | |
|---|---|
| AZKABAN | QUIDDITCH |
| CUPBOARD | ROWLING |
| DRACO | SECRET |
| DIAGON ALLEY | SNAPE |
| GOBLET | SORTING HAT |
| HAGRID | SPELL |
| HERMIONE | VOLDEMORT |
| HOGWARTS | WAND |
| MAGIC | WITCH |
| MUGGLES | WIZARD |

```
Y F I R S T D A N C E
O C U R E O U P R M G
O M H G M M A X U Y A
B E D A A I E F E T S
H U N K P L R H E D R
B B E I G E G E T F O
S U E T P P R C L A C
P P U N C H B O W L S
R N Q T Y W W M N E H
E R W E Y E K M N E O
D E C O R A T I O N S
U N L S G L O T N K N
E T A D O R W T S G O
M A N B S Y P E E O P
L E T H G I N E T A L
```

BAND
BUDGET
CHAPERONES
COMMITTEE
CORSAGE
DATE
DECORATIONS
FIRST DANCE
FLOWERS
GOWN

KING
LATE NIGHT
LIMO
MAKEUP
PERFUME
PUNCH BOWL
QUEEN
SENIORS
THEME
TUXEDO

# UPS AND DOWNS

```
P E G A S P R I C E S
O L T D E V O A U E L
P S K I J U M P E R S
O T E V K R S S F O A
G N D E L E A H T L A
O Y P R F W R U O L Y
S T O C K M A R K E T
T G P Y R N L D A R A
I Y E R O S A L G C I
C F O R T U N E S O R
K L T S A I Y R O A P
G S O N V S D U P S L
A N U S E H T E A T A
N D D R L T O W N E N
T E M P E R A T U R E
```

| | |
|---|---|
| AIRPLANE | POP FLY |
| ASTRONAUT | ROLLER COASTER |
| DIVER | SEESAW |
| ELEVATOR | SKI JUMPERS |
| FORTUNES | STOCK MARKET |
| GAS PRICES | TEMPERATURE |
| GEYSER | TENT |
| HURDLER | THE SUN |
| KITE | TIDE |
| POGO STICK | YO-YO |

For instructions on how to solve Guess the Theme puzzles, see page 7. The word list is on page 67.

```
S K E B V C E R Y G W
O E B R O K E N N R D
C E I F A A N I G O B
E P F L W A R M I N G
F E O R F A E D O R A
E R S F E T E R I T H
M A I L O R D E R N D
E W C O A S R D H L G
T A O B C U S T O M S
O U U S S M G H R E T
W O N F T M O H E R W
M H T W A E N O T O T
H E I R W R A O R E R
D F N T O R P K O H R
E R G R E E N A P S E
```

B _ _ _ _ _ _ _
B _ _ _
B _ _ _ _ _
C _ _ _ _ _ _ _
C _ _ _ _ _
C _ _ _ _ _ _ _
C _ _ _ _ _ _
F _ _ _ _
G _ _ _ _
H _ _ _

K _ _ _ _ _
M _ _ _ - _ _ _ _ _
P _ _ _ _ _
S _ _ _ _ _ _ _ _
S _ _ _ _
S _ _ _ _ _
W _ _ _ _ _ _
W _ _ _ _
W _ _ _
W _ _ _

# GRADUATION DAY

```
T  I  F  H  U  G  S  V  W  E  H
N  U  K  O  O  B  R  A  E  Y  M
E  A  N  W  S  G  T  L  E  Y  A
M  Y  N  O  M  E  R  E  C  T  M
E  T  S  H  A  E  E  D  P  R  O
C  S  P  R  I  N  C  I  P  A  L
N  K  S  I  N  M  S  C  F  P  P
E  L  E  S  S  A  T  T  O  P  I
M  O  R  T  A  R  B  O  A  R  D
M  R  U  R  G  C  O  R  R  E  A
O  D  T  U  O  H  E  I  A  K  T
C  I  C  N  G  N  W  A  N  A  H
A  A  I  T  T  D  O  N  O  E  S
H  E  P  S  E  P  G  H  E  P  S
C  L  A  S  S  R  I  N  G  S  T
```

| | |
|---|---|
| CAPS | PARENTS |
| CEREMONY | PARTY |
| CLASS RING | PICTURES |
| COMMENCEMENT | PRINCIPAL |
| DIPLOMA | SENIORS |
| GOWN | SPEAKER |
| HONOR | TASSEL |
| HUGS | TEARS |
| MARCH | VALEDICTORIAN |
| MORTARBOARD | YEARBOOK |

```
T  R  U  O  C  D  O  O  F  T  A
L  L  P  A  A  E  S  W  O  R  B
A  U  R  L  S  R  A  W  E  A  S
S  T  A  R  B  U  C  K  S  P  C
S  R  H  A  T  W  C  A  L  A  O
Y  N  T  E  O  O  H  E  D  G  W
A  C  S  E  L  B  R  A  M  E  S
D  T  L  T  G  I  W  A  R  H  D
I  U  O  A  N  L  M  C  L  T  L
R  O  A  T  I  S  J  I  T  S  A
F  G  S  H  K  R  H  A  T  T  N
I  N  S  R  R  M  E  O  A  E  O
G  A  L  L  A  M  R  S  P  A  D
T  H  J  C  P  E  N  N  E  Y  C
L  L  N  O  R  D  S  T  R  O  M
```

ARCADE
BROWSE
CARTS
CLAIRE'S
FOOD COURT
FOOT LOCKER
HANG OUT
J.C. PENNEY
J. CREW
MARBLES

MCDONALD'S
NORDSTROM
PARKING LOT
SEARS
SHOP
STARBUCKS
STORE
T.G.I. FRIDAY'S
THE GAP
THE LIMITED

# ZERO HOUR

The list below contains words meaning "nothing" and phrases with the word "nothing." In the grid, though, when the word "nothing" appears, we've replaced it with an O. Thus, GOOD-FOR-NOTHING will appear as GOODFORO. When two words cross at a shared O, it may act as the letter O in one word and "nothing" in the other.

```
T H I N K O O F I T O
T H U O E Z S I F T F
O L C H O E I E M M O
L B G I S R L L U E Y
G I U N N O F O C E T
O Y L T I D R W H H N
O T A O T O I T A S E
S R D E F R D S D C L
E A R D R E O O O L P
E P O A U S Q U A T T
G O I L E B E T B D O
G W C N A W A S O L G
A O S H A O O O U W E
N N A B O D U T T T V
O K K C I L A T O N I
```

GOOD-FOR-NOTHING
GOOSE EGG
"I'VE GOT PLENTY OF NOTHING"
KNOW-NOTHING PARTY
MUCH ADO ABOUT NOTHING
NADA
NO CLUE
NO HINT
NOT A LICK
NOTHING AT ALL

NOTHING BUT TROUBLE
NOTHING DOING
NOTHING LEFT
NOTHING TO IT
NOTHING TO WEAR
NULL
SQUAT
"THINK NOTHING OF IT"
ZERO
ZILCH

# CARRY ON!

```
W  G  A  B  L  E  F  F  U  D  F
E  H  O  R  G  A  S  G  H  E  S
S  C  E  R  R  A  R  R  C  R  R
A  I  A  E  E  E  P  R  U  P  E
C  B  I  T  L  O  T  G  O  P  L
F  E  O  E  H  B  Y  R  P  N  I
E  S  H  L  A  D  A  V  O  E  A
I  B  L  L  D  E  E  R  O  P  R
R  E  R  A  E  B  H  C  R  O  T
B  E  C  W  N  T  U  S  A  O  E
D  S  T  O  E  M  N  O  G  A  W
C  I  O  K  N  A  V  C  N  S  E
Y  L  S  M  E  R  S  S  A  A  G
F  A  N  N  Y  P  A  C  K  R  E
B  V  S  G  A  B  K  O  O  B  T
```

| | |
|---|---|
| BARGE | PORTER |
| BASKET | PRAM |
| BELLHOP | PURSE |
| BOOK BAG | SACK |
| BRIEFCASE | TORCHBEARER |
| CADDY | TRAILER |
| CART | VALISE |
| DUFFEL BAG | WAGON |
| FANNY PACK | WALLET |
| KANGAROO POUCH | WHEELBARROW |

```
V V O W E L S W H E B
E A L O E F C F C O S
C O N T E S T A N T E
O R T N T U T U S N Z
E E N E A E S I S H I
R V B I G W I N N E R
H B L O P A H S E D P
Y O R O N S B I T A U
M Y H E S O U L T D Z
E C R L A E Y S S E Z
T T O P K C A J S I L
I C U G A J U T M E E
M O N B A N K R U P T
E F D K H A N G M R A
N I S T H E R E A N N
```

BANKRUPT
BIG WINNER
BONUS
"... BUY A U"
CASH
CATEGORY
CONTESTANT
"IS THERE AN N?"
JACKPOT
LETTER

LOSE A TURN
PAT SAJAK
PRIZES
PUZZLE
RHYME TIME
ROUND
SOLVE
SPIN
VANNA WHITE
VOWELS

# ALL FIRED UP

```
F F H D R O H W O S S
S G O L E Y V E A P L
E T O R D E M B E R F
W Z K R E R T O T I M
F L A M E S E N R N B
O N N L O K T E I K S
T B D I B M M F U L R
N Y L G E A T B I E F
E O A H N T S B U R N
O L D T K C S E C S E
A N D N O H T K H Y B
W I E N I E R O A S T
E K R I A A L M L T A
E D B Y P C F S I E R
F A L S E A L A R M E
```

ASHES
BLAZE
BURN
CANDLE
EMBER
FALSE ALARM
FIREMAN
FLAMES
FLINT
FOREST FIRE

HOOK AND LADDER
HYDRANT
LIGHT
LOGS
MATCH
SMOKE
SPARK
SPRINKLER SYSTEM
WARM
WIENIE ROAST

# SUITS ME FINE

$\mathsf{A}$ deck of cards has four suits: clubs (♣), diamonds (♦), hearts (♥), and spades (♠). The symbols for these suits appear in the grid in place of the words for suits in the word list. For example, CLUB SODA would appear as ♣SODA.

```
♥  T  O  ♥  T  A  L  K  S  ♠  A
M  E  ♠  ♣  G  A  P  V  W  E  ♠
A  B  V  S  ♦  R  U  O  I  A  N
♣  A  M  A  R  D  R  G  ♠  R  T
Y  S  O  N  R  K  P  A  H  I  I
R  E  S  D  S  B  L  S  W  Z  ♥
T  B  E  W  E  L  E  T  ♠  O  ♥
N  A  A  I  A  ♠  ♥  T  F  N  T
U  L  ♣  C  ♦  H  D  G  E  A  I
O  L  N  H  I  H  O  I  G  ♦  H
C  ♦  E  G  O  L  F  ♣  V  B  T
♣  A  F  P  D  U  ♥  E  K  A  T
D  O  E  R  A  ♣  S  S  T  C  D
E  ♦  J  U  B  I  L  E  E  K  A
K  B  R  E  A  K  O  N  E  S  ♥
```

ARIZONA DIAMONDBACKS
BASEBALL DIAMOND
BRAVEHEART
BREAK ONE'S HEART
CALL A SPADE A SPADE
CLUBHOUSE
CLUB SANDWICH
COUNTRY CLUB
DAVID SPADE
DIAMOND HEAD

DIAMOND JUBILEE
DRAMA CLUB
GOLF CLUB
HEART OF GOLD
HEART-TO-HEART TALK
HOPE DIAMOND
IN SPADES
PURPLE HEART
SPADEWORK
TAKE HEART

# COME FLY WITH ME

```
T L U G G A G E C T O
N R N N A N S N A C K
A E A I M A I K B E N
D H S Y A S E D I S C
N L O L T O L V N S L
E E C F F A O C T A E
T D L F O M B V E P L
T M O O R G E L I G R
A T U R T W O R E N T
T H D A R W T O L I P
H O X E U D I U S D A
G I N F N D C N A R L
I I R U W S K I D A C
L K O N A E E S E O S
F R B A Y G T M S B W
```

| | |
|---|---|
| AISLE | MOVIE |
| BOARDING PASS | PILOT |
| CABIN | ROUND TRIP |
| CLOUD | RUNWAY |
| FEAR OF FLYING | SNACK |
| FLIGHT ATTENDANT | TAKEOFF |
| LANDING | TAXI |
| LEGROOM | TICKET |
| LUGGAGE | TRAY TABLE |
| MEAL | WINDOW |

```
C H A R I O T B H I F
N F M O T R T O I Y I
Y S B R E A T R J K R
S O U C A R R I A G E
N C L B O E T S L L E
K T A D L N U N I T N
S M N A E O N B M W G
E L C Y C R O T O M I
L R E E S M C H K E N
C D O I W U V E C R E
Y T W O G O L T H S O
C I N W A H S K C I R
I S X U S A N N Y D C
N A R A H A N S O M S
U S K A T E B O A R D
```

| | |
|---|---|
| AMBULANCE | RICKSHAW |
| BIKE | SCHOOL BUS |
| CARRIAGE | SKATEBOARD |
| CHARIOT | SLEIGH |
| FIRE ENGINE | SNOWMOBILE |
| HANSOM | SULKY |
| HOT ROD | TANK |
| JITNEY | TAXI |
| LIMO | TRUCK |
| MOTORCYCLE | UNICYCLE |

```
M  B  U  K  I  M  M  U  R  O  R
E  A  O  M  O  N  E  L  T  Y  C
I  L  S  G  S  C  A  R  I  L  E
A  D  T  O  G  E  G  D  U  F  S
Y  E  R  F  O  L  N  E  S  E  E
R  R  M  O  U  S  E  T  R  A  P
Y  D  A  M  K  O  J  U  U  N  C
S  A  O  N  P  C  T  O  P  L  H
C  S  H  Y  O  S  A  T  L  T  E
R  H  H  T  S  I  A  R  A  N  C
A  B  E  E  Z  Y  T  B  I  T  K
B  H  U  S  E  E  O  C  V  S  E
B  G  U  S  S  O  E  M  I  I  R
L  T  W  I  S  T  E  R  R  P  S
E  N  C  O  N  N  E  C  T  4  T
```

| | |
|---|---|
| BALDERDASH | PICTIONARY |
| BOGGLE | RACK-O |
| CHECKERS | RISK |
| CHESS | RUMMIKUB |
| CLUE | SCRABBLE |
| CONNECT 4 | SORRY! |
| GUESSTURES | TABOO |
| JENGA | TRIVIAL PURSUIT |
| LIFE | TWISTER |
| MOUSE TRAP | YAHTZEE |

# THE ONE RING

```
            S  H  I  R  E  I
         A  C  F  Y  F  T  B  O  U  F
      I  R  I  N  G  W  R  A  I  T  H  S
   N  O  W  D  M  O  R  D  O  R  L  T  H  S
   M  E  E  T  T           D  R  B  G  A
I  I  L  N  O              O  O  O  M  G
Y  T  D  W                 U  L  G  S
A  H  E  L                 L  L  A  E
Y  R  G  O                 U  U  M  V
S  I  A  O                 R  M  G  L
H  L  E  G  R              O  R  A  E  E
   O  E  N  O  L        N  B  N  O  E
   R  B  H  T  R  A  E  E  L  D  D  I  M  E
   D  B  O  S  N  B  F  T  A  H  E  R
   P  I  H  S  W  O  L  L  E  F
      T  I  N  F  G  S
```

| | |
|---|---|
| ARAGORN | HOBBIT |
| ARWEN | MIDDLE-EARTH |
| BALROG | MITHRIL |
| BILBO | MORDOR |
| ELVES | ORCS |
| ENTS | RINGWRAITHS |
| FELLOWSHIP | SAM GAMGEE |
| FRODO | SAURON |
| GANDALF | SHIRE |
| GOLLUM | TWO TOWERS |

```
M A M I N U T E M E N
S Y S S E R G N O C B
T E M N L Y I H S U O
A G A R L T I M N E S
O R I L A O I K O D T
C O L O N I E S N I O
D F T O A R G N N R N
E Y S O H T R E A T Y
R E N I T A O G C H T
S L L T E P E R E G R
L L L A B O G U Y I A
W A S H I N G T O N P
T V T F R A N C E D A
H E B R I T I S H I E
W A R S T E K S U M T
```

ARMY
BOSTON
BRITISH
BUNKER HILL
CANNONS
COLONIES
CONGRESS
ETHAN ALLEN
FRANCE
KING GEORGE III

MIDNIGHT RIDE
MINUTEMEN
MUSKETS
PATRIOT
REDCOATS
TEA PARTY
TORY
TREATY
VALLEY FORGE
WASHINGTON

# "ACHOO!"

```
M  G  A  L  D  A  N  D  E  R  M
C  O  M  M  O  N  C  O  L  D  S
R  D  L  O  S  T  O  H  S  A  P
I  B  L  D  L  S  V  N  O  E  R
A  L  R  E  P  P  E  P  H  O  E
F  E  U  E  S  E  R  A  N  E  A
O  S  Z  F  N  E  Y  R  E  L  D
T  S  U  D  E  F  O  S  L  K  G
S  Y  S  H  E  C  U  E  L  C  E
R  O  U  V  Z  T  R  T  O  I  R
U  U  E  H  E  G  M  O  P  T  M
B  R  E  I  Y  R  O  E  F  Y  S
T  I  E  H  D  N  U  S  E  G  E
S  N  O  I  T  A  T  I  R  R  I
T  H  G  I  L  T  H  G  I  R  B
```

| | |
|---|---|
| "ACHOO!" | "GOD BLESS YOU" |
| ALLERGY | HAY FEVER |
| BRIGHT LIGHT | IRRITATION |
| BURST OF AIR | MOLD |
| COMMON COLD | NOSE |
| "COVER YOUR MOUTH!" | PEPPER |
| DANDER | POLLEN |
| DUST | SNEEZE |
| FORCEFUL | SPREAD GERMS |
| "GESUNDHEIT!" | TICKLE |

# THIS IS Z END

```
Z  A  N  Z  I  B  A  R  Z  S  N
O  O  E  O  O  C  R  T  Z  B  N
F  R  E  O  R  R  L  A  L  R  O
O  O  Z  A  K  A  R  I  Z  T  Z
D  E  Z  S  W  Z  Z  O  S  I  Z
R  Y  A  H  T  Z  E  E  L  C  L
A  I  K  E  A  L  Z  T  E  O  E
Z  T  I  R  F  E  H  T  N  O  C
I  E  D  Y  N  D  Z  A  J  T  G
W  C  P  O  Z  A  H  A  S  A  A
E  H  Z  P  I  Z  Z  A  Z  Z  Z
H  O  I  R  E  Z  U  A  T  M  G
T  H  A  Z  E  L  L  F  O  O  I
M  Z  E  Z  Z  E  I  B  M  O  Z
C  N  O  Z  A  M  A  N  Z  Z  S
```

| | | |
|---|---|---|
| AMAZON | JAZZ | WHIZ |
| A TO Z | KAZOO | YAHTZEE |
| AZALEA | NOZZLE | ZANZIBAR |
| AZTEC | ON THE FRITZ | ZEPPELIN |
| BLIZZARD | OOZE | ZERO |
| BRAZIL | OZONE | ZEST |
| CRAZY | PIZZAZZ | ZIGZAG |
| CZAR | RAZZLE-DAZZLE | ZOMBIE |
| FUZZY | THE WIZARD OF OZ | ZOOM |
| HAZEL | WALTZ | ZORRO |

## 0 | GUESS THE THEME 1

| | |
|---|---|
| BAR CODE | OLD MOVIE |
| CHESS PIECES | ONE-WAY SIGN |
| COWS | ORCA |
| CROSSWORD PUZZLE | PANDA |
| DICE | PENGUIN |
| DOMINO | PIANO KEYS |
| EIGHT BALL | SKUNK |
| JOLLY ROGER | SNOOPY |
| MIME | X-RAY |
| NUN'S HABIT | ZEBRA |

## 24 | GUESS THE THEME 2

| | |
|---|---|
| ARTILLERY | PIANO |
| BOULDER | REFRIGERATOR |
| BREATHING | SCHEDULE |
| BURDEN | SNOWFALL |
| CREAM | STEP |
| FREIGHT | TAXES |
| HEART | THINKER |
| HITTER | TRAFFIC |
| LOAD | TRUCK |
| METAL | WHALE |

# 44 GUESS THE THEME 3

| | |
|---|---|
| BOARDING | KEEPER |
| BOAT | MAIL-ORDER |
| BROKEN | PORTER |
| CLEARING | SLAUGHTER |
| COFFEE | STEAK |
| COUNTING | SUMMER |
| CUSTOMS | WARMING |
| FLIES | WHITE |
| GREEN | WIFE |
| HOLD | WORK |

# 1 | GETTING STARTED

Driver's advice: Engage mind before putting mouth in gear.

# 2 | WELL-GROOMED

U.S. bathrooms inspired me more than European cathedrals. [paraphrase of Edmund Wilson]

## 3 | PEANUTS GALLERY

Woodstock the bird's speech is made mostly of vertical hash marks.

## 4 | "TAKE A HIKE!"

When you want someone to leave you alone, tell him or her to take a hike.

## 5 | LIFE OF E'S

Eve feeds eleven elves sweets except when Everest freezes.

## 6 | THE ROMAN EMPIRE

Mountain water flowed downhill via nine aqueducts to ancient Rome.

# 7 AT THE BALLET

Some football pros take ballet to help get more flexible.

# 8 GUESS THE THEME 1

All the hidden things are known for being black and white.

# 9 | ELECTION DAZE

"Vote early and often" was a slogan in some very corrupt U.S. elections.

# 10 | "WHAT'S THE POINT?"

If you reach your boiling point, are you then at the point of no return?

## 11 MONEY MATTERS

How can money go out so fast when it comes in so slowly? [paraphrase of a quip by Ogden Nash]

## 12 FAST JUNK

Jokers say the basic food groups are chocolate, fat, sugar, and salt.

# 13 | ART CLASS

Old cliché: I don't know anything about art but I know what I like.

# 14 | ORDER IN THE COURT!

The NBA star Shaquille O'Neal has a Superman tattoo on one arm.

## 15 WATCH YOUR LANGUAGE

Deaf people use sign language, which is made up of gestures, not speech.

## 16 OPPOSITES ATTRACT

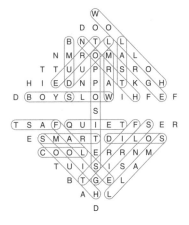

Don't think different is bad.

**"IT'S A MYSTERY!"**

Nancy Drew is still young after seventy years solving cases.

 **BIRTHDAY PARTY**

You have a birthday, and each April there's an Earth Day.

# 19 ONE OF A KIND

Eat a well-done T-bone steak in Indonesia.

# 20 SEA FOR YOURSELF

Some boat names are Noah's Ark, Titanic, and Gilligan's Minnow.

## 21 HINKY PINKIES

My guy gave the moose juice and the bear care.

## 22 IN WONDERLAND

"Twinkle, twinkle, little bat! How I wonder what you're at!" [recited at the Mad Tea Party]

## 23 | SIX-LETTER BOYS

Oh boy, what a bunch of boys' names!

## 24 | GUESS THE THEME 2

The puzzle theme here is things that are associated with being heavy.

# 25

## "HAIR WE GO!"

Human hair grows twenty percent faster in the summer than in winter.

# 26

## SNOWBOARDING

The term for small young snowboarders is "grommets," or "groms" for short.

## 27 | A CLOTHES CALL

Wearing expensive clothes doesn't mean having good taste in them.

## 20 | MARCHING BAND

Those who do not keep pace may hear a different drummer.

## 29 SEEING STARS

Did you read your horoscope? It says don't believe everything you read.

## 30 IN THE DRIVER'S SEAT

Most road rage incidents occur on hot days.

# ANSWERS

## 31 | GARDEN PARTY

"A man of words and not of deeds is like a garden full of weeds."—by Mother Goose

## 32 | ROUND AND ROUND

Other round things are wheels, bubbles, polka dots, pies, scoops of ice cream, Frisbees, and buttons.

## 33 | "A-MAZE-ING!"

If you go along this path, you'll go in the right direction, so don't stop now!

## 34 | BEDTIME

At slumber parties it's more fun to stay up late than to slumber.

## 35 | "I'M THANKFUL FOR ..."

Life is not fair. Be thankful for what you have, and do the best you can.

## 36 | LOOKIN' GOOD

If you miss a cosmetics quiz, do you have to take a makeup test?

## 37 FOOTBALL FUN

Most years, the most-viewed TV show in the U.S. is the Super Bowl.

## 38 STAGESTRUCK

In Shakespeare's age, men played all the parts—the male and female.

## 34   SHOE THING

Imelda Marcos once had more than a thousand pairs of shoes.

## 40   HIGH SCHOOL TEAMS

A good team pulls together; a bad one pulls apart.

## 41 HARRY POTTER

There are seven hundred ways to commit a foul in a quidditch game.

## 42 AT THE PROM

Your prom may be the biggest party where you'll know so many people.

## 43 — UPS AND DOWNS

Pole-vaulters and leapfrog players also go up and down.

## 44 — GUESS THE THEME 3

Every word can go before or after the word HOUSE to form another word or phrase.

## 45 GRADUATION DAY

If we humans get sheepskins for graduating, what do sheep get?

## 46 AT THE MALL

Tall Paul saw a scrawl on the wall at that small mall.

## 47 ZERO HOUR

The sitcom "Seinfeld" was described as a show about nothing.

## 48 CARRY ON!

For ages, carrier pigeons have been used to convey messages.

## 49 WHEEL OF FORTUNE

"Wheel of Fortune" is based on the old classic game of hangman.

## 50 ALL FIRED UP

F.D. Roosevelt wrote, "Books burn . . . yet . . . books cannot be killed by fire."

## 51 — SUITS ME FINE

Sam Spade gave a diamond ring to his sweetheart at the nightclub for a club steak.

## 52 — COME FLY WITH ME

One man has collected over two thousand airsickness bags.

# LAND ROVERS

In forty years, one stuntman wrecked over two thousand cars.

# GAME TIME

More money is created for Monopoly than by the U.S. Mint.

## 55 THE ONE RING

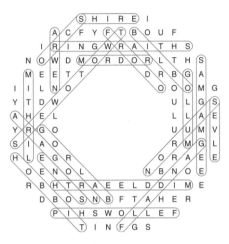

If you find the trilogy dull, you're bored of the rings.

## 56 IT'S REVOLUTIONARY

Many "Hamilton" songs tell about the war.

## 57 "ACHOO!"

Almost all sneezers shut their eyes.

## 58 THIS IS Z END

Snoozers like to catch some zzz's.